Cincinnati
Our City, Our Story

This book is dedicated to the families in our tri-state region.
May you always encourage and enjoy reading and exploration.

by Louise Borden
Illustrations by Children of Greater Cincinnati
A collaborative of the Cincinnati Storyteller's Project
benefiting Every Child Succeeds

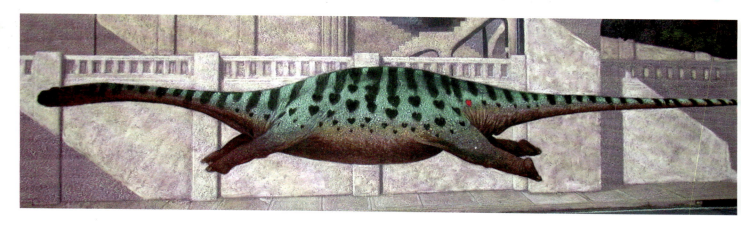

blue manatee press
Cincinnati, Ohio

First Edition: Fall, 2012.

Library of Congress Cataloging-in-Publication Data

Borden, Louise.
Cincinnati - Our City, Our Story / by Louise Borden—1st ed.
Summary: A guided tour of greater Cincinnati, and its people,
places, and history. Art provided by area children showcases community
and civic pride, inviting families to explore the region. A collaborative
project by a subgroup of the Cincinnati USA Regional Chamber
C-Change 7 class, benefiting local non-profit Every Child Succeeds.
ISBN-13 (hardcover): 978-1-936669-11-0
ISBN-13 (paperback): 978-1-936669-12-7
Printed in the USA

Cincinnati is our city
and our story.
It's the place we call home.

From quiet streets
to busy avenues,
our families come together
with one proud voice:

"Cincinnati."

Say it again . . .

"Cincinnati!"

Zoe
Age 9

3

Become an explorer,
a Cincinnati explorer . . .
Bring your family along, too,

and go north,
south,
east
or west.
The compass of our city
tells our story.

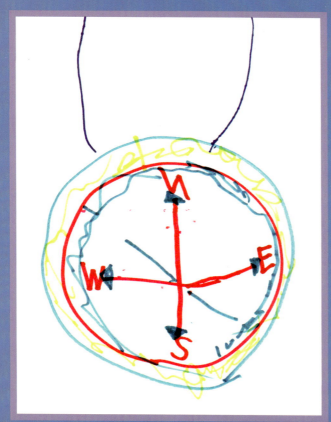

"It's easy.
We spell it like this:

Cin

cin

nati."

Grace
Age 11

5

Long ago
our city was not a city at all . . .

Tori
Age 9

Only hills and forests,
creeks and streams

and paths worn smooth
by the hunters of Ohio's tribes.

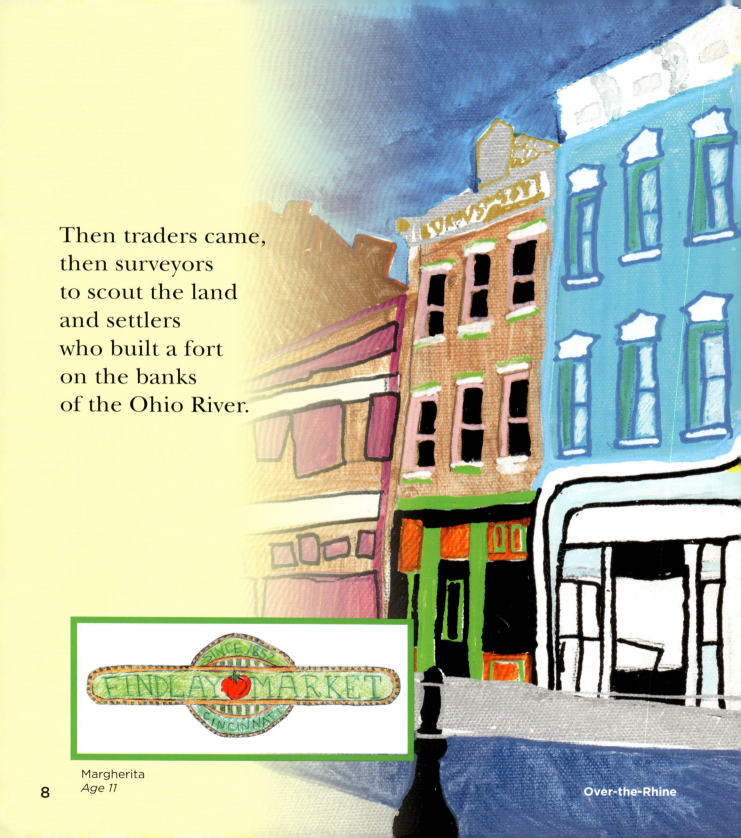

Then traders came,
then surveyors
to scout the land
and settlers
who built a fort
on the banks
of the Ohio River.

Margherita
Age 11

Over-the-Rhine

Leah
Age 10

Then down those waters
came the maps
for our new country,
in flatboats
carrying cows and pigs
and brave pioneers
with big ideas.

Some families were
from Germany,
an old country
far away.
That's
why we have streets
and food
with echoes of
German names.

9

And before there were bridges or cars in Cincinnati,
we crossed our river on ferryboats
that were poled
from bank to bank
and back again
because Covington and Newport
and northern Kentucky
are part of our story too.

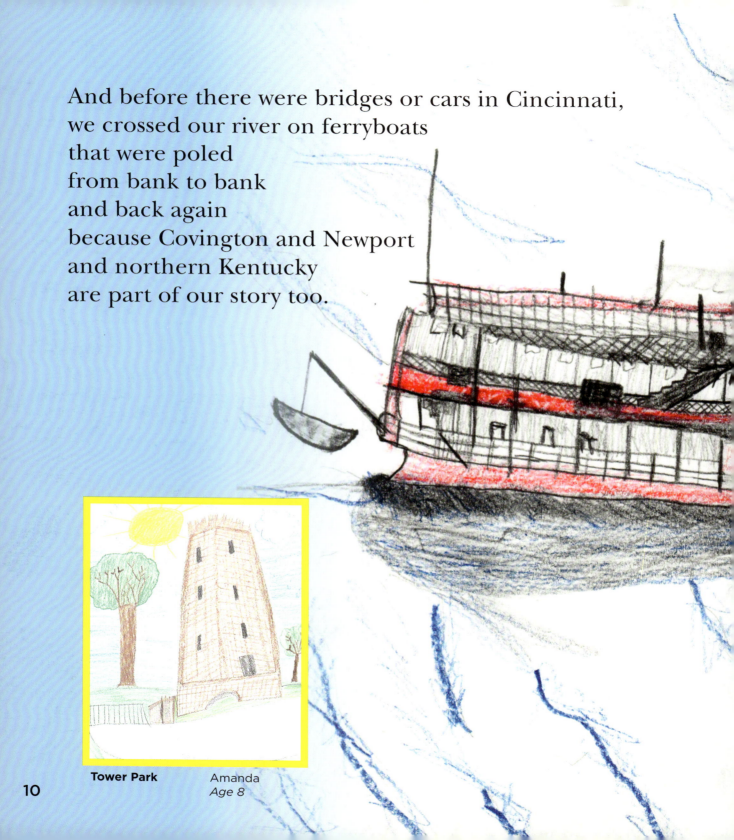

Tower Park
Amanda
Age 8

Come ride on a modern ferry
and listen to the chug of its engine.
Two states . . . minutes apart
and linked by water.

Lucy
Age 11

During the Civil War
our city stood on the side
of the North
and helped slaves
cross our Ohio River to
freedom.

Jaydn
Age 9

Dmarco
Age 10

One by one
our downtown buildings
grew tall
to shape our city's skyline.

Up

up

up

Forty-nine stories on an elevator -
Wow, what a view!
See the world made small
in our Cincinnati.

Trevor
Age 9

Look down
to find the
heart of our city . . .

Celebrations!
Speeches!
Holidays!
Parades!

Emma
Age 12

And don't forget to cross
our beautiful bridges.
Oh those bridges!
Can you count them?

They too
are part of our story.

Blue
or yellow
or purple
or silvery gray.
Our bridges span our river . . .
Ohio to Kentucky,
and Kentucky to Ohio.

Caroline
Age 11

Look up and see the sky.
Look across and see our hills.
Look down and
and watch the swirl of current
carry the long barges
slowly past.

Our river.
Our city.
Our region.

Cincinnati!

17

18　　Garrison
Age 12

Eric
Age 9

The game of baseball
came down that muddy Ohio too
with a bat or a glove
packed in a trunk
on a paddle wheeler.

Because our Cincinnati
is the city of baseball.
We're the home of the **Cincinnati Reds.**

"Peanuts! Popcorn!"

And if you're lucky,
fireworks will shower the sky

"A home run!"
"He's rounding third and heading for home . . ."

20

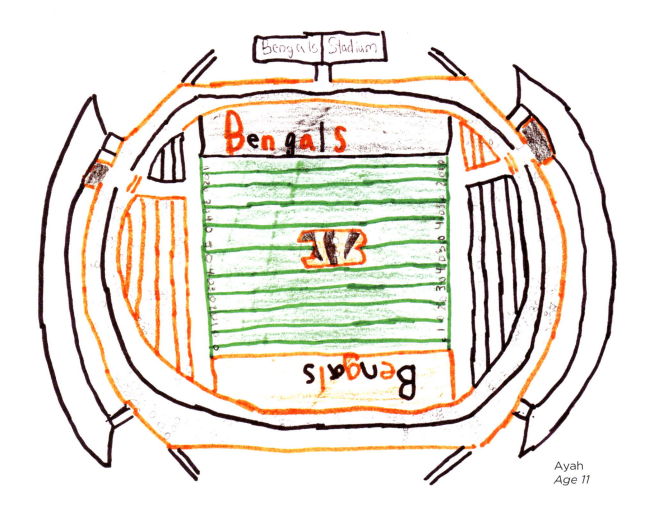

Ayah
Age 11

And don't forget those **Bengals!**
Oh those fearsome **Bengals**
who play in rain or snow or shine.

Touchdown!

Hurray for our teams!
Hurray for our city!

Snow
Age 13

Noor
Age 11

Noor
Age 11

As explorers
you can be the first to tell others
we are many small stories
within one big story:

Artists and printers
and soapmakers
and doctors and musicians
and teachers and farmers
and actors and scientists
and pilots and carpenters
and gardeners
and firemen and writers

Lily
Age 10

Astrid
Age 13

and even two **presidents**
of our country.

And you can tell others
that we have many places to discover
within one great city.

So check your compass:
and head north or south,
east or west . . .

Cincinnati!

Contemporary Arts Center

Maya
Age 10

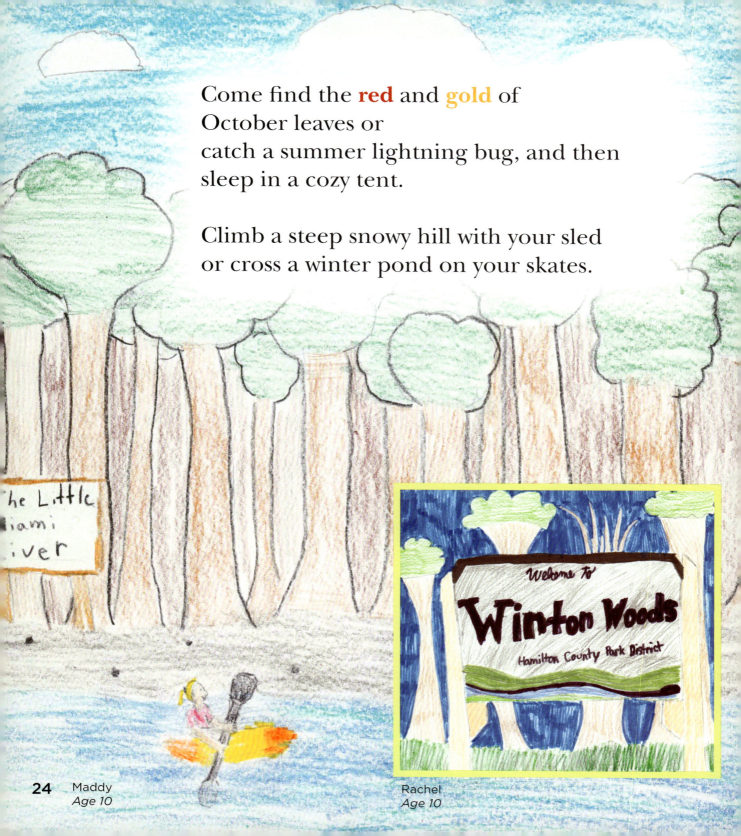

Come find the **red** and **gold** of
October leaves or
catch a summer lightning bug, and then
sleep in a cozy tent.

Climb a steep snowy hill with your sled
or cross a winter pond on your skates.

The Little
iami
iver

Welcome to
Winton Woods
Hamilton County Park District

24   Maddy
      Age 10

Rachel
Age 10

Or like an astronomer,
study the moon

or count the stars

with the oldest working telescope
in America.

Brian
Age 9

The Cincinnati Observatory

Make a list of parks to explore
all over our map.

Cincinnati!

Mia
Age 11

Hurry downtown
or chart a new neighborhood:

then carry home
your favorite books.

Or check out a new title
to read with someone who loves you.

Zack
Age 12

Cotton candy?

Any time of day —

so hop into a rollercoaster
car.

Hear it inch to the very top

until
you
can
only
see
the
sky . . .

then . . .

WHOOOOOSH

down the rails.

Hold on to your hat
for an explorer's ride!

27

Eden Park
Kendall
Age 11

Art Museum
Josie
Age 9

Can you map the curvy roads

that lead to the lake
that shines like a mirror?

Or that end at the museum
where famous paintings hang on walls?

Grace
Age 11

Do *you* have a nickname?

Our city,
our terrific city,
has more than one.

Because **Cincy** is quicker to say than Cincinnati,
and **Porkopolis** inspired our flying pigs,
and the **Queen City** tells the world how special we are.

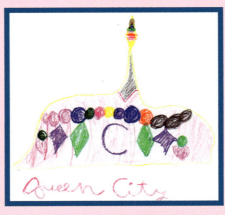

Clo
Age 6

Now here come the little **airplanes**
and the sleek fast jets
rising high into the sky.

Stand by the fence,
watch the pilots take off and land
and wave to the clouds above.

Shey
Age 9

CINCINNATI ZOO & BOTANICAL GARDEN

Chelsie
Age 10

Gabrielle
Age 9

**But don't forget the zoo.
Oh, our wonderful zoo!**

With our amazing white tigers!
With our snakes and giraffes!

Hurry,
see them all on a hot summer day.

or bundle up in explorer mittens
to marvel at the lights
that shine in the wintry night.

33

Loveland Castle

Find a castle
(yes, a castle)

or pack a picnic
and then go for a swim in a gigantic pool.

Mary
Age 12

Newport Aquarium

James
Age 9

Cross a bridge to Kentucky
and see schools of fish
of every color
and find a shark too.

Caroline
Age 8

Music Hall

Daniella
Age 10

Next, hold on to your compass
and hear the years of **music**
fill this majestic hall.

Just blocks away,
count the stair-steps of water
by our grand station
for travelers and trains.

Buy your tickets for the big screen . . .
or to learn about something old
or new.

But first

look up . . .

look up . . .

Such a huge rotunda!

Listen to your voices echo.
Stand tall with pride.

We're the luckiest ones
because Cincinnati
and its Kentucky side, too,
belong to all of us.

North and south,
east and west,

uptown and downtown,
across town,
or on the way to town.

Over those bridges
and under those stars,

we have places to explore
and a story to tell.

Our story. Our city.

Cincinnati!

Allison
Age 10

THANK YOU TO OUR SUPPORTERS!

Organizers
Sub-committee of C-Change, Class 7 of the Cincinnati USA Regional Chamber.   Lyndsey Barnett (Co-Chair) - Graydon Head & Ritchey LLP; Lindsey Riehl (Co-Chair) - Cincinnati Museum Center at Union Terminal; Aaron Hoffman – Michelman, Inc.; Jason Kershner - Cincinnati USA Regional Chamber; Heather Muzumdar - Thompson Hine LLP; Craig Nolte – dunnhumbyUSA; Matt Reckman - US Bank; David Robertshaw - Turner Construction

Creative Talents
ArtWorks/Brent Lakes, Louise Borden, blue manatee/Dr. John S. Hutton, Loren Long, OMS Photography/TJ Vissing, C.F. Payne, Scooter Media, Will Hillenbrand

Matching Grant
Smale Family Foundation

Major Donors

Members of C-Change, Class 7 - The C.J. Krehbiel Company - Dr. John Hutton & Sandra Gross - The Seven Hills Group at Morgan Stanley Smith Barney LLC - The Lois and Richard Rosenthal Foundation

Donors
Agenda 360 - Cincinnati Museum Center at Union Terminal - Graydon Head & Ritchey LLP Haverkamp Riehl & Michel Co. LPA - Johnson Investment Counsel - Keating Muething & Klekamp PLL - LaRosa's, Inc. - Michelman, Inc - Thompson Hine LLP - Turner Construction Company Vorys, Sater, Seymour and Pease LLP

Illustration Selection Panel
Cincinnati Public Library: Charlene Bandurraga-Hole, Sam Bloom, Lorie Bonapfel, Mary Ann Culbertson, Carolyn Janssen, Mary Watring

Submitting Schools
Bevis Elementary – Cincinnati Country Day School – Hilltop Elementary School – Indian Hill Elementary & Middle Schools Little Miami Intermediate & Junior High – Mariemont Elementary – Monfort Heights Elementary - Mother Teresa Catholic Elementary - Our Lady of Visitation - Oyler School - Reading Hilltop Elementary – Sands Montessori - Seipelt Elementary Silverton Paideia Elementary – St. Gertrude – St. Ignatius Loyola School – Summit Country Day – Summit View Elementary Terrace Park Elementary – The New School Montessori – The Seven Hills School – Xavier University Montessori

Caroline
Age 9

Riverfront Fireworks